ALLEN WILCOX

FOUR-HAND PIANO MUSIC

by Nineteenth-Century Masters

FOUR-HAND PIANO MUSIC

by Nineteenth-Century Masters

EDITED BY
MOREY RITT

DOVER PUBLICATIONS, INC.
New York

PREFACE AND ACKNOWLEDGMENTS

Performance of music for four hands at one piano, although frequently perceived as the province of amateurs, is to all pianists a challenge, and at times a vexing one: problems of balance, pedalizations and fingering are abundant. In the interest of presenting an uncluttered score and in accordance with Debussy's admonition, "Cherchons nos doigtées" (let us look for our fingerings), the editor has added neither performance suggestions nor fingerings. Measure numbers have been added for convenience where not previously present.

Pianists familiar with nineteenth-century piano duet literature, and therefore surprised by the almost total absence of four-hand music by Schubert and Brahms, should note that this repertoire is available in other Dover volumes.

I would like to thank my colleagues Professor Saul Novack, whose recommendation initiated my participation in this publication, and Professor Barbara Greener, who made available the impressive resources of the Music Library at Queens College. I am also grateful to Jill Schnall, Ann Ritt, Werner Loewenstein and Joseph and Constance Goodman, all of whom made vital contributions.

MOREY RITT

Published in Canada by General Publishing Company, Ltd., 30 Lesmill Road, Don Mills, Toronto, Ontario.
Published in the United Kingdom by Constable and Company, Ltd.

Four-Hand Piano Music by Nineteenth-Century Masters is a new selection of works, first published by Dover Publications, Inc., in 1979. The music has been reproduced from the following sources:

[Beethoven] *Ludwig van Beethoven's Werke. Vollständige kritisch durchgesehene überall berechtigte Ausgabe.* Series 15; B.123. Breitkopf & Härtel, Leipzig, n.d.

[Schubert] *Franz Schubert's Werke. Kritisch durchgesehene Gesammtausgabe.* Series 9, No. 19; F.S.79. Breitkopf & Härtel, Leipzig, 1888.

[Mendelssohn] *Felix Mendelssohn Bartholdy's Werke. Kritisch durchgesehene Ausgabe von Julius Rietz.* Series 10; M.B.48. Breitkopf & Härtel, Leipzig, n.d. (complete edition published between 1874 and 1877).

[Schumann] *Robert Schumann's Werke. Herausgegeben von Clara Schumann.* / Breitkopf & Härtel, Leipzig, 1887. (*Bilder aus Osten:* Series 6, No. 2; R.S.35. / *Zwölf vierhändige Clavierstücke:* Series 6, No. 3; R.S.36.)

[Bizet] *Jeux d'enfants* / 12 pièces pour piano à quatre mains / *Edition originale,* Editions Durand & Cie, Paris, n.d.

[Dvořák] *Společnost Antonína Dvořáka.* Series 5; H592, H1801, H2153, respectively, Státní Nakladatelství Krásné Literatury, Hudby a Umění, Prague, ca. 1955–57.

[Debussy] *Petite Suite / Pour / Piano à quatre mains,* Durand & Cie, Paris, n.d.

[Fauré] *Dolly / Op. 56 / pour piano à 4 mains,* Hamelle et Cie, Paris (reprint of original publication of 1894).

The selection and the Notes on the Music have been prepared specially for the present edition by Morey Ritt.

International Standard Book Number: 0-486-23860-1
Library of Congress Catalog Card Number: 79-52205

Manufactured in the United States of America
Dover Publications, Inc.
180 Varick Street
New York, N.Y. 10014

CONTENTS

NOTES ON THE MUSIC

LUDWIG VAN BEETHOVEN
(1770–1827): Song, "Ich denke dein," with Six Variations, WoO 74

In his *Life of Beethoven*, Thayer relates the following history of the variations on "Ich denke dein":

> On May 23, 1799, Beethoven wrote in an album for his two young pupils [Countesses Josephine and Therese Brunsvik, the dedicatees of the work] a song in D on Goethe's text, 'Ich denke dein,' and four variations on it for four hands. Four years later he added two more variations; and the third sister, Charlotte, wrote to Josephine on September 9, 1803: '. . . Savez-vous déjà que Beethoven a composé encore deux variations dans notre stambuch. N'est-il pas bien aimable, et adorable . . .?' (Do you already know that Beethoven has composed two more variations in our album. Isn't he kind and charming?)

These last two variations became the third and fourth in the published version. Pianists may wonder why Charlotte Brunsvik did not mention that the fourth, as published, is considerably more challenging than the other variations.

Beethoven used as text the opening stanza of Johann Wolfgang von Goethe's poem "Nähe des Geliebten" (Presence of the Loved One). The translation is as follows: "I think of you when I see the gleam of the sun reflected in the sea; I think of you when the flickering of the moon is painted on the fountains."

FRANZ SCHUBERT
(1797–1828): Divertissement à la hongroise (Hungarian Divertimento), Op. 54

From the year of its composition, 1824, through our own time this extraordinary work has elicited divided critical opinion. Schumann noted in his diary on October 9, 1836 that Mendelssohn, hearing the piece, "stamped his feet" with impatience. A recent biographer of Schubert, Maurice Brown, contributes his own negative reaction: "Many of Schubert's faults are present . . . but we find few of his virtues." Liszt, however, thought well enough of the work to arrange portions for piano solo (*Mélodies hongroises [d'après Schubert]*, written in 1838–39) and for orchestra (*Vier Märsche von Franz Schubert*, written in 1859–60). Of these four marches, two are from Op. 54, the others from Opp. 40 and 121. Curiously, Liszt later transcribed these four marches once again, this time for piano duet!

The *Hungarian Divertimento* is, indeed, magnificent; bold, consistently imaginative and replete with melodic invention, it is unique in the duet literature.

FELIX MENDELSSOHN
(1809–1847): Andante and Variations, Op. 83a

In his biography of Mendelssohn, *On Wings of Song*, Wilfrid Blunt quotes a letter of July 15, 1841 from the composer to Karl Klingemann in which Mendelssohn excitedly reports:

> Can you guess what I've just been composing—and passionately? Variations for piano! Eighteen of them on a theme in D minor [the *Variations sérieuses*, Op. 54], and I had such enormous fun with them that I immediately went on to some on a theme in E flat, and now I'm on my third on one in B flat. It's just as though I had to make up for lost time in never having written any before.

This third set (Op. 83), often dismissed as lacking in substance, particularly when compared to the Op. 54 variations, was rewritten as a piano duet in the same year. Amazingly, the duet transcription, written so soon after the original, presumably with little time for reflection, far exceeds it in breadth, color and formal interest. This phenomenon was to recur, but in reverse, in 1843 when Schumann, having composed his *Andante and Variations*, Op. 46, for two pianos, two 'celli and horn, then revised the work for two pianos. Schumann thus facilitated performance but, unfortunately, also sacrificed much that was beautiful in form, substance and timbre.

ROBERT SCHUMANN
(1810–1856): Bilder aus Osten (Pictures from the East): Six Impromptus, Op. 66

Schumann wrote the following preface to the original edition of this work which he composed in 1848:

> The composer of the pieces that follow believes they will be better understood if he declares that they owe their creation to a particular stimulus. In fact, the pieces were written during the reading of Rückert's *Makamen* (tales from the Arabic of Hariri); the marvelous hero of the book, Abu Seid—who could be compared to our German Till Eulenspiegel, except that Abu Seid is a far more poetical and noble conception—as well as the figure of his honorable friend Hareth, occupied the composer's mind incessantly during the writing of the music; this may explain the exotic character of some of the pieces. Nevertheless, the composer did not envision specific incidents of the stories in the first five pieces, and only the last one might perhaps be considered to be a reflection of the last *Makame*, in which we see the hero end his merry life in regret and penance. So then, may this attempt to express Eastern ways of artistic creation and thought in approximate fashion in the art of music, as has already been done in German poetry, be received not unfavorably by my sympathizers.

Al-Hariri was a scholar who lived in Basra from ca. 1054 to ca. 1122. The German poet and Orientalist Friedrich Rückert (1788–1866) adapted Al-Hariri's *Makamat* in 1823–24, publishing it as *Die Verwandlungen des Abu Seid von Serug, oder die Makamen des Hariri* (The Metamorphoses of Abu Seid of Serug, or The Tales of Al-Hariri). Rückert's work was highly praised by Thomas Carlyle, who called it a "jewel" and wrote: "I cannot tear myself away from it."

Modern scholars have also made much of the literary background of *Bilder aus Osten.* Kathleen Dale states that this work "stands alone . . . among all Schumann's complete sets of individual pieces for the keyboard, either solo or duet, in having been *avowedly* composed in response to a single definite literary stimulus."

Such statements and the strong initial impact made on Schumann by exotic scenes he observed during his trip to Russia in 1844 and by his meeting with Rückert while en route might well lead to the conclusion that *Bilder aus Osten* strongly reflects a number of extramusical influences. However, as is often the case, such influences have been considerably subordinated to the exigencies of musical creation.

SCHUMANN:
AM SPRINGBRUNNEN (AT THE FOUNTAIN) AND ABENDLIED (EVENING SONG)

Schumann's *Album für die Jugend* (Album for the Young) of 1848 had been so well received that his publisher Schuberth planned to issue a second edition in 1851. Therefore he asked Schumann to compose a set of duets of similar character that could be published at the same time as the new edition of *Album für die Jugend.* Schumann complied immediately, the twelve pieces being completed in September 1849.

The charming title of the opus notwithstanding, "Am Springbrunnen" is certainly not for children, except for prodigies or the eternally young in heart. Schumann directs that it be played as quickly as possible; at such speed, and with delicacy to match, it is a feathery, delightful tour de force.

"Abendlied" is brief, serene and one of the most beautiful pieces of the set.

GEORGES BIZET
(1838–1875): JEUX D'ENFANTS (CHILDREN'S GAMES)

In *Jeux d'enfants* and *Dolly,* Bizet and Fauré, in company with other Romantic composers, cast sentimental glances toward an idealized, poetic childhood. Emile Vuillermoz, in a discussion of *Dolly* that is also pertinent to *Jeux d'enfants,* states that Romantic "tenderness before the cradle" was of "relatively recent vintage. The Classicists, and for sterner reasons, the Primitives, had no knowledge of it. . . . These

tokens of homage interest children less than their parents. It is among adults that one exchanges amusing and tender observations and knowing winks."

Winton Dean, however, makes a valid distinction between degrees of sentimentality. Describing *Jeux d'enfants,* he writes: "Here is a typically French wit and detachment combined with a warmth and sympathy that recall Schumann without the adult nostalgia of the *Kinderscenen.*"

Of the twelve pieces (see the Table of Contents for full titles and translations), Nos. 2, 3, 6, 11 and 12 were also arranged for orchestra by Bizet and published in 1882 as *Petite Suite d'orchestre.* Both versions were composed in 1871, however, and the question of which was chronologically first has not been entirely resolved, although it seems likely that the ten duets commissioned by Durand (Nos. 7 and 8 being added later) had priority, with the orchestral potentialities being quickly appreciated and realized. In one instance, however, we can be certain that the duet version was a transcription: No. 6, "Trompette et tambour," was taken from a march originally written for Bizet's opera *Ivan IV,* even the revision of which antedated *Jeux d'enfants* by six years.

ANTONÍN DVOŘÁK
(1841–1904): SLAVONIC DANCE, OP. 46, NO. 5; LEGEND, OP. 59, NO. 6; SILENT WOODS, OP. 68, NO. 5

Simrock, Dvořák's publisher, suggested to him in 1878 that he write a set of Slavonic dances similar in style to Brahms's *Hungarian Dances.* Dvořák worked quickly. The eight *Dances,* Op. 46, were begun on March 18 and completed on May 7; between April and August of the same year they were also orchestrated by the composer. That acclaim promptly followed publication is shown by the following excerpt from a review written during the same year by Louis Ehlert for the Berlin *Nationalzeitung:* "Here at last is a one hundred-percent talent and, what is more, a completely natural talent. I consider the *Slavonic Dances* to be a work that will make its triumphant way through the world in the same way as Brahms's *Hungarian Dances.* . . . Whoever finds a jewel on the public highway is under obligation to report his find. I beg the reader to look upon these lines from that point of view."

The ten *Legends,* composed in February and March of 1881, were orchestrated later in the same year by Dvořák. Eduard Hanslick, to whom they were dedicated, wrote: "Perhaps this one is the most beautiful of all the ten *Legends,* perhaps another one is; about that there will be different opinions, within the general verdict that they are all beautiful." Brahms wrote in a letter to Simrock: "Tell Dvořák how his *Legends* continue to charm me. That is a delightful work and one envies the fresh, cheerful and rich resourcefulness of the man."

Unlike the *Dances* and *Legends*, the six pieces *From the Bohemian Forest*, composed in 1883 and 1884, were not orchestrated. "Silent Woods," however, reappeared in 1891 as a work for 'cello and piano and in 1893 as a 'cello solo with orchestral accompaniment. A humorous addition to the history of Op. 68 is provided by Marie Červinková-Riegrová, the librettist of two of Dvořák's operas, who wrote that while planning this suite, the composer was more concerned with naming the pieces than with musical problems; he complained to her that Schumann had used up most of the suitable titles!

CLAUDE DEBUSSY
(1862–1918): Petite Suite (Little Suite)

Although Debussy traveled in 1888 to Bayreuth, where he heard Wagner's operas *Parsifal* and *Die Meistersinger*, no musical evidence of such exposure exists in this popular suite composed during the same year.

Debussy and his publisher, Jacques Durand, collaborated in the first performance on March 1, 1889. Unfortunately, acceptance of the work was to come only later; in a letter Durand wrote: "The audience was completely indifferent. I was heartbroken." *Petite Suite* was later orchestrated, not by Debussy but by Henry Büsser, then a young student at the Paris Conservatoire.

This work, so poised, so obviously in possession of the charm, clarity and detachment prized by generations of French musicians, is seen in perspective to have been more of a farewell than could have been imagined by Debussy and his French contemporaries. At this time Richard Strauss was composing his tone poems; just a few years in the future were the overwhelming emotionality and orchestrations of Gustav Mahler and the young Arnold Schoenberg. Chronologically at one with these developments, though stylistically antithetical, were Debussy's *Prélude à l'après-midi d'un faune* (1894) and Ravel's *Jeux d'eau* (1901). With Debussy leading the way in orchestral music and Ravel in writing for the piano, musical Impressionism was created. Original and pervasive, if short-lived, this style honored the traditions and preserved the identity of French music while new talents and directions were emerging elsewhere in Europe.

GABRIEL FAURÉ
(1845–1924): Dolly, Op. 56

Fauré began work on *Dolly*, a suite of six pieces, in 1893 and completed the set three years later, dedicating it to an evidently charming child, Dolly Bardac. The tranquil scenes that formed the environment of her existence are reflected in the titles. "Mi-a-ou" was the name of the household kitten. Vuillermoz interprets No. 3 as a portrayal of a young girl's grace and innocent flirtatiousness; in No. 6 he visualizes Dolly in Spanish costume, dancing while accompanying herself on a tambourine. These pieces were orchestrated not by Fauré but by Henri Rabaud, then a young composer soon to be appointed conductor of the Paris Opéra and Opéra-Comique.

Dolly, the fortunate if unwitting recipient of Fauré's homage, was the daughter of Emma Bardac. In 1905 Mme. Bardac married Claude Debussy and in 1908 musical history was repeated when Debussy wrote *Children's Corner* for another charming young girl, their daughter, the "dear little Chouchou" to whom he dedicated this famous suite of piano pieces.

BIBLIOGRAPHY

Basch, Victor. *Schumann: A Life of Suffering*, trans. Catherine Alison Phillips. New York, 1931.

Blom, Eric, ed. *Grove's Dictionary of Music and Musicians*. New York, 1954.

Blunt, Wilfrid. *On Wings of Song*. New York, 1974.

Brown, Maurice. *Schubert: A Critical Biography*. New York, 1977 (reprint of 1958 ed.).

Clapham, John. *Antonín Dvořák, Musician and Craftsman*. New York, 1966.

Dale, Kathleen. "The Piano Music," in *Schumann, A Symposium*, ed. Gerald Abraham. London, 1952.

Dean, Winton. *Georges Bizet: His Life and Work*. London, 1965.

Long, Marguerite. *At the Piano with Debussy*, trans. Olive Senior-Ellis. London, 1972.

Rückert, Friedrich. *Rückerts Werke*, ed. Georg Ellinger. Leipzig, n.d.

Thayer, Alexander. *Life of Beethoven*, ed. Elliot Forbes. Princeton, 1967.

Vuillermoz, Emile. *Gabriel Fauré*, trans. Kenneth Schapin. Philadelphia, 1960.

GLOSSARIES

GLOSSARY OF GERMAN TERMS IN THE SCHUMANN PIECES

Ausdrucksvoll und sehr gehalten: with expression and very sustained
Erster Spieler: first player (primo)
Erstes Tempo: original tempo
Etwas langsamer: somewhat more slowly
Etwas lebhafter: somewhat more briskly
Etwas zurückhaltend: holding back somewhat
Im Tempo: back in tempo
Im Volkston: like a folksong
Lebhaft: briskly

Mit Verschiebung: soft pedal
Nach und nach etwas belebter: gradually becoming somewhat livelier
Nicht schnell (und sehr gesangvoll zu spielen): not fast (and very cantabile)
Noch schneller: faster yet
Reuig andächtig: penitently and piously
Schneller: faster
So schnell als möglich: as fast as possible
Zweiter Spieler: second player (secondo)

GLOSSARY OF FRENCH TERMS IN THE BIZET AND DEBUSSY PIECES

augmentez et animez: crescendo, livelier tempo
aussi . . . que possible: as . . . as possible
brillant: brillante
croisez: cross hands
détaché: staccato
encore plus retenu: holding back even more
en retenant peu à peu: gradually holding back
fin: end
gracieux: gracefully
la basse en dehors: bringing out the bass line
le chant très marqué et très expressif: the melody very marcato and espressivo
lentement: slowly

mouv[emen]t de marche: march time
Mouv[emen]t de Valse à un temps: one-beat waltz time
naïvement: naïvely
Ôtez la P[eti]te Pédale: release soft pedal
Petite Pédale: soft pedal
pressez: accelerando
retenu: holding back
soutenu sans lourdeur: sustained without heaviness
toujours détaché: maintain the staccato
très rythmé: very rhythmically
un peu retenu: holding back a little

FOUR-HAND PIANO MUSIC

by Nineteenth-Century Masters

SONG, "ICH DENKE DEIN," WITH SIX VARIATIONS,
WoO 74, by Ludwig van Beethoven

SECONDO.

Ich den _ ke ____ dein, wenn mir der Son _ ne Schim _ mer von

Mee _ ren ____ strahlt, ich den _ _ ke dein, wenn sich des Mon _ des

Flim _ mer in Quel _ len malt.

SONG, "ICH DENKE DEIN," WITH SIX VARIATIONS,
WoO 74, by Ludwig van Beethoven

Var. I.

SECONDO.

Var. II.

PRIMO.

SECONDO.

Var.III.

PRIMO.

Var. IV.

Var. V.

Var. VI.

Coda.

PRIMO.

DIVERTISSEMENT À LA HONGROISE, OP. 54
by Franz Schubert

DIVERTISSEMENT À LA HONGROISE, OP. 54
by Franz Schubert

Secondo.

Primo.

Secondo.

Primo.

Secondo.

Secondo.

Primo.

Secondo.

Primo.

MARCIA.
Andante con moto.

Trio.

Fine.

D.C.

MARCIA.
Andante con moto.

Primo.

Secondo.

Primo.

Secondo.

Primo.

Secondo.

Primo.

Primo.

Secondo.

Secondo.

Primo.

Secondo.

Primo.

Secondo.

Primo.

Secondo.

Primo.

Secondo.

44 Franz Schubert

Primo.

Divertissement à la hongroise 45

Secondo.

Primo.

ANDANTE AND VARIATIONS, OP. 83a
by Felix Mendelssohn

SECONDO.

Andante tranquillo con Variazioni.

ANDANTE AND VARIATIONS, OP. 83a
by Felix Mendelssohn

PRIMO.

SECONDO.

VAR. II. Animato.

PRIMO.

VAR. II. Animato.

PRIMO.

VAR. III.

VAR. IV.

VAR. IV.

SECONDO.

Felix Mendelssohn

SECONDO.

Felix Mendelssohn

SECONDO.

VAR. VIII. Allegro molto agitato.

Felix Mendelssohn

PRIMO.

VAR. VIII. Allegro molto agitato.

SECONDO.

PRIMO.

SECONDO.

Felix Mendelssohn

Allegro assai vivace.

SECONDO.

Felix Mendelssohn

PRIMO.

Andante and Variations 67

SECONDO.

Felix Mendelssohn

PRIMO.

BILDER AUS OSTEN, OP. 66, by Robert Schumann

I.

BILDER AUS OSTEN, OP. 66, by Robert Schumann

I.

II.

Nicht schnell und sehr gesangvoll zu spielen.

II.

Nicht schnell und sehr gesangvoll zu spielen.

III.

III.

IV.

IV.

Nicht schnell.

V.

V.

VI.

Reuig andächtig.

Nach und nach etwas belebter.

Reuig andächtig.

VI.

Nach und nach etwas belebter.

TWO PIECES FROM "ZWÖLF VIERHÄNDIGE CLAVIERSTÜCKE," OP. 85, by Schumann

Am Springbrunnen.

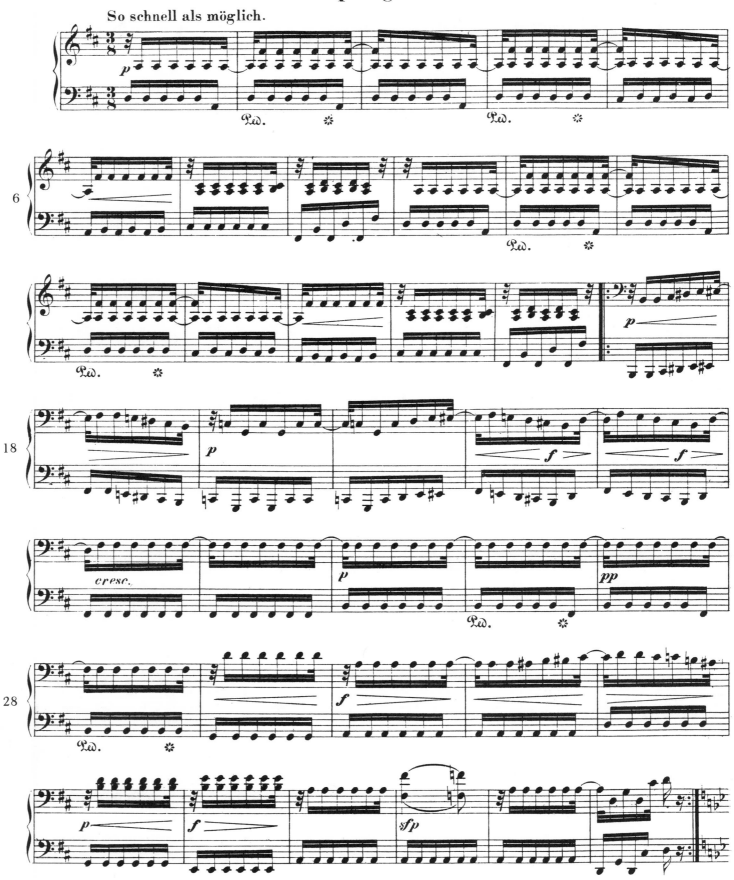

TWO PIECES FROM "ZWÖLF VIERHÄNDIGE CLAVIERSTÜCKE," OP. 85, by Schumann

Am Springbrunnen.

So schnell als möglich.

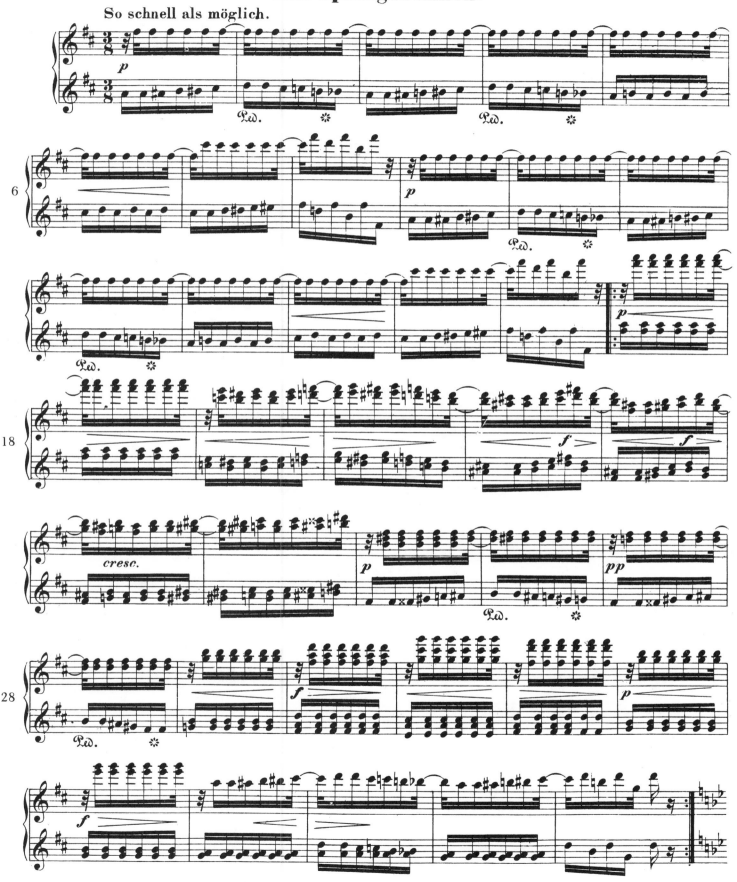

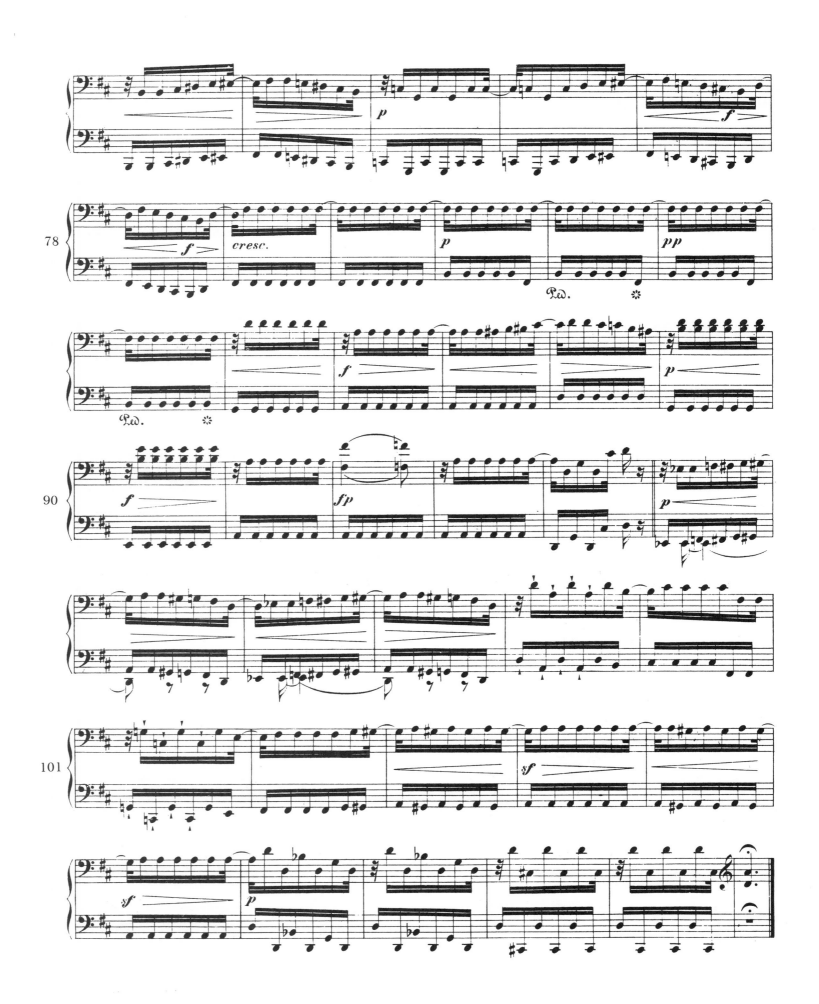

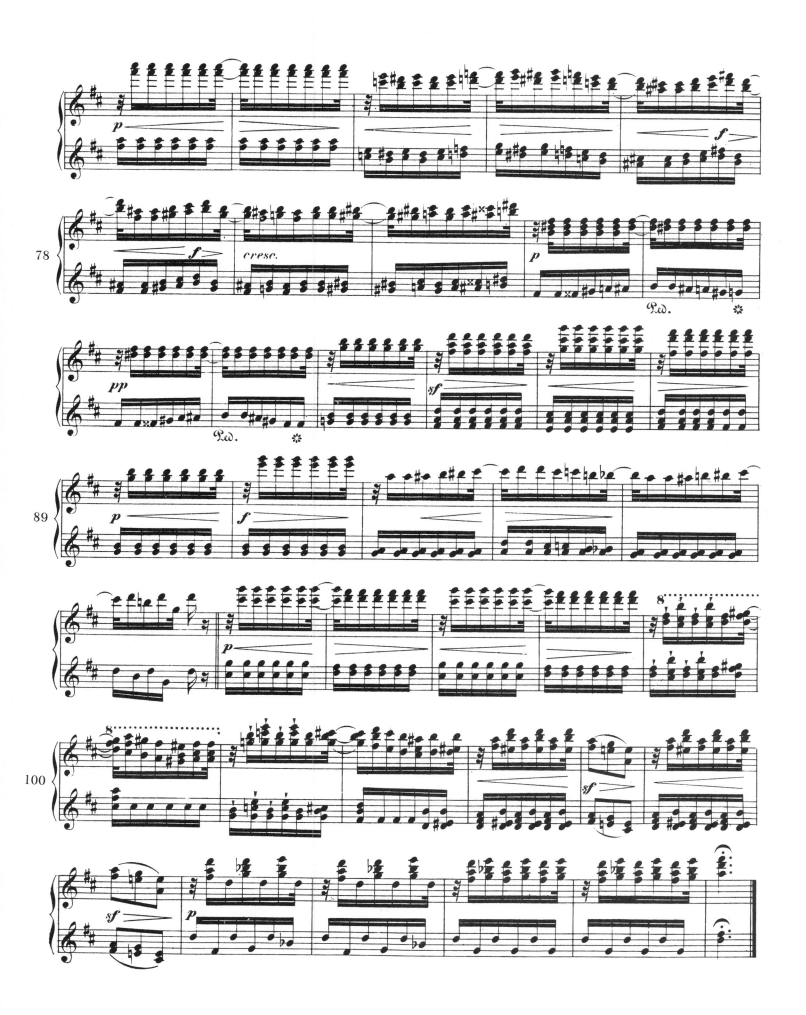

Abendlied.

Ausdrucksvoll und sehr gehalten.

Abendlied.

JEUX D'ENFANTS, by Georges Bizet

L' ESCARPOLETTE

REVERIE.

SECONDA

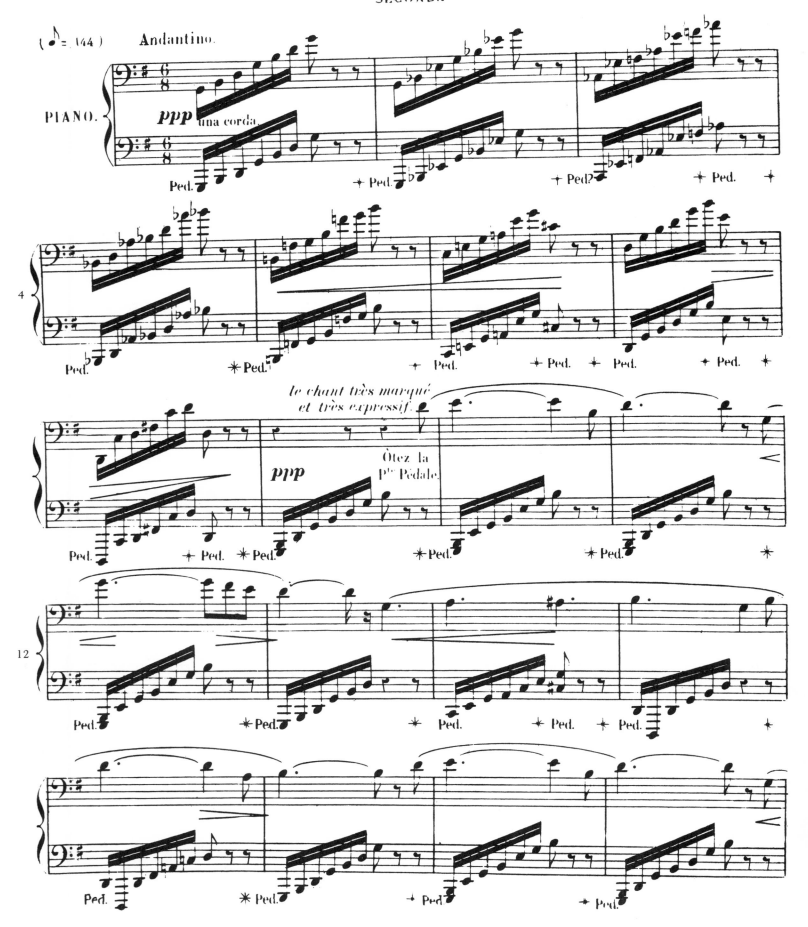

JEUX D'ENFANTS, by Georges Bizet

L'ESCARPOLETTE

REVERIE.

PRIMA.

PRIMA.

PRIMA.

Jeux d'enfants 107

LA TOUPIE

IMPROMPTU

SECONDA.

LA TOUPIE

IMPROMPTU

SECONDA.

LA POUPÉE

BERCEUSE.

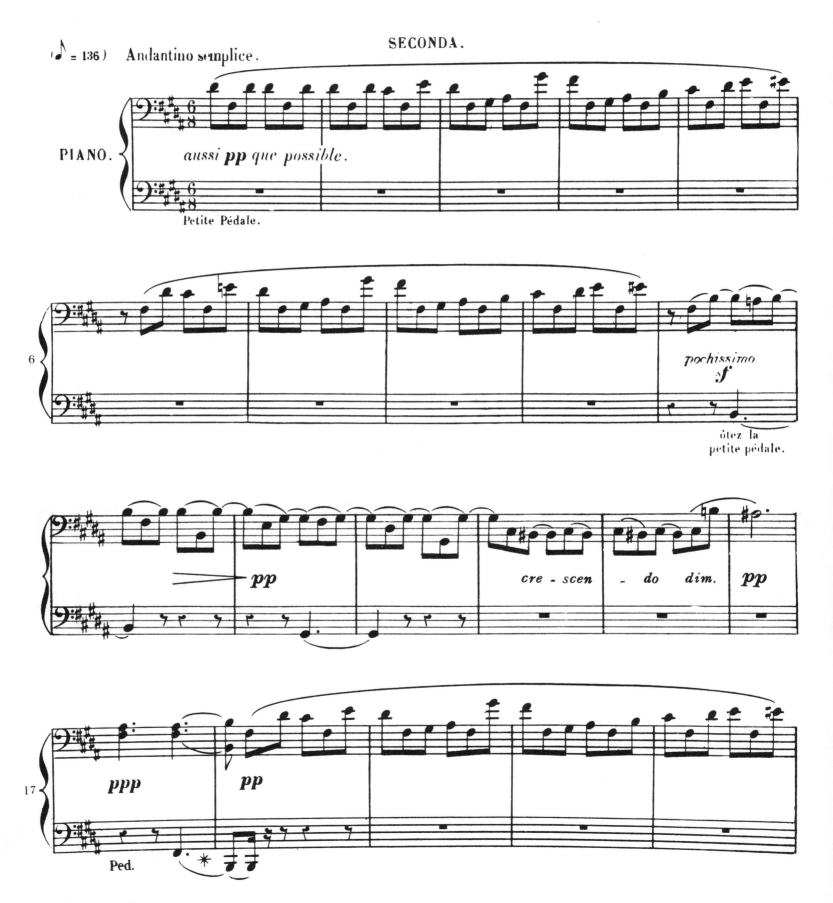

aussi **pp** que possible.

Petite Pédale.

pochissimo *ƒ*

ôtez la
petite pédale.

cre - scen _ do dim. **pp**

ppp   **pp**

Ped.

LA POUPÉE

BERCEUSE.

PRIMA.

SECONDA.

LES CHEVAUX DE BOIS

SCHERZO

LES CHEVAUX DE BOIS

SECONDA.

Georges Bizet

Jeux d'enfants 119

120   Georges Bizet

PRIMA.

LE VOLANT

FANTAISIE.

SECONDA.

LE VOLANT

FANTAISIE.

TROMPETTE ET TAMBOUR

MARCHE.

SECONDA.

TROMPETTE ET TAMBOUR

MARCHE.

PRIMA.

PRIMA.

LES BULLES DE SAVON

RONDINO.

SECONDA.

Allegretto moderato.

LES BULLES DE SAVON

RONDINO.

PRIMA.

SECONDA.

LES QUATRE COINS

ESQUISSE.

SECONDA.

LES QUATRE COINS

ESQUISSE.

PRIMA.

SECONDA.

PRIMA.

140   Georges Bizet

PRIMA.

SECONDA.

142   Georges Bizet

PRIMA.

Jeux d'enfants 143

COLIN-MAILLARD

NOCTURNE.

SECONDA.

COLIN-MAILLARD

NOCTURNE.

PRIMA.

PRIMA.

SAUTE - MOUTON

CAPRICE.

SECONDA.

SAUTE - MOUTON

CAPRICE.

PETIT MARI, PETITE FEMME!..

DUO.

SECONDA.

PETIT MARI, PETITE FEMME!..

DUO.

PRIMA.

PRIMA.

LE BAL

GALOP.

LE BAL

GALOP.

PRIMA.

SLAVONIC DANCE IN A MAJOR, OP. 46, NO. 5
by Antonín Dvořák

Allegro vivace

SLAVONIC DANCE IN A MAJOR, OP. 46, NO. 5
by Antonín Dvořák

168   Antonín Dvořák

LEGEND IN C-SHARP MINOR, OP. 59, NO. 6
by Antonín Dvořák

LEGEND IN C-SHARP MINOR, OP. 59, NO. 6
by Antonín Dvořák

Tempo I.

PRIMO

"SILENT WOODS," OP. 68, NO. 5
by Antonín Dvořák

"SILENT WOODS," OP. 68, NO. 5
by Antonín Dvořák

186   Antonín Dvořák

PETITE SUITE, by Claude Debussy

I. EN BATEAU

PETITE SUITE, by Claude Debussy

I. EN BATEAU

194   Claude Debussy

a tempo

en retenant

peu a peu

encore plus retenu

II CORTÈGE

II CORTÈGE

III MENUET

III. MENUET

SECONDA

IV. BALLET

IV. BALLET

PRIMA

I°. Tempo

DOLLY, OP. 56, by Gabriel Fauré

Nᵒ 1
Berceuse

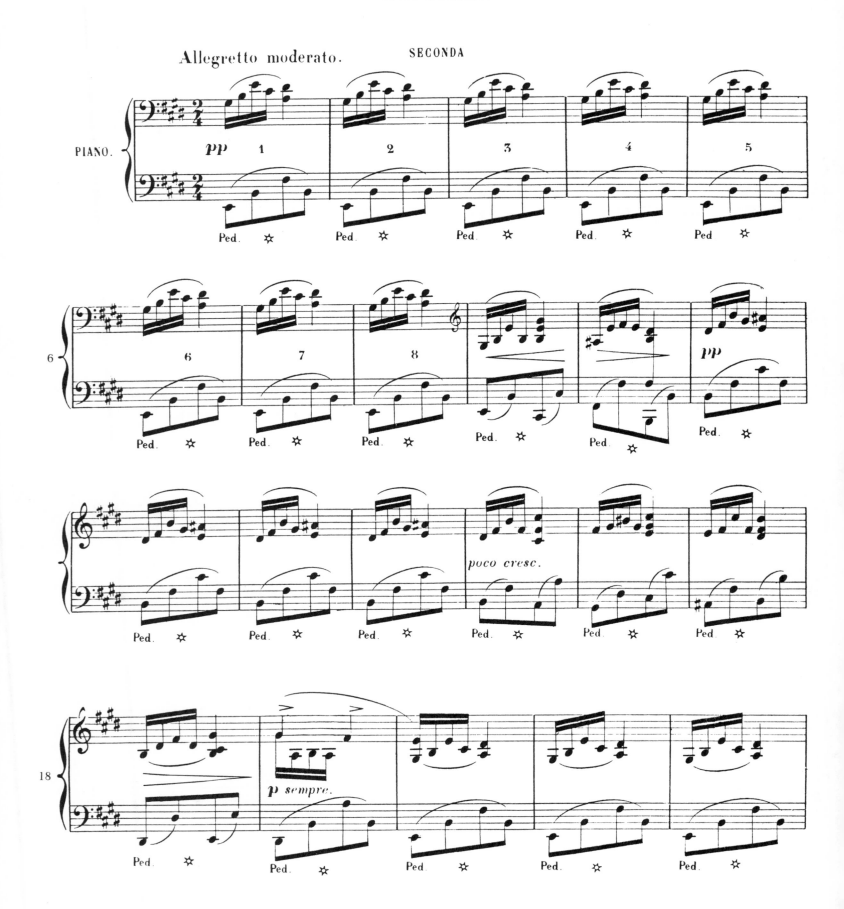

DOLLY, OP. 56, by Gabriel Fauré

№ 1
Berceuse

PRIMA

Dolly 223

N° 2
Mi-a-ou

N° 2
Mi-a-ou

nᵒ 3
Le jardin de Dolly

N° 3
Le jardin de Dolly

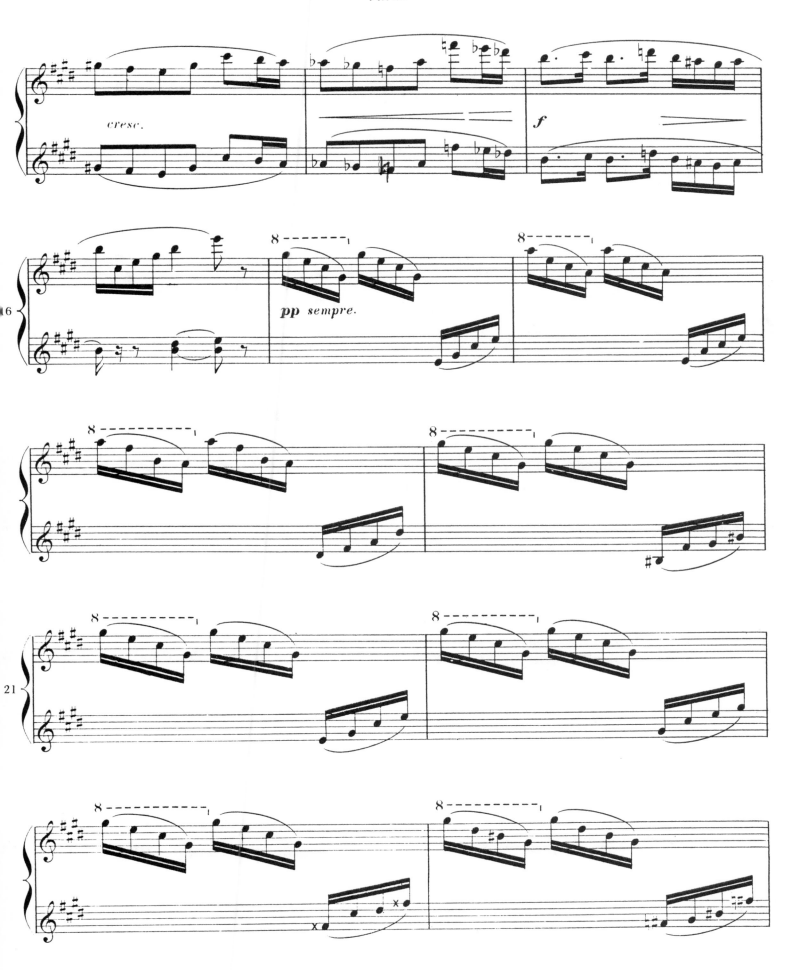

240   Gabriel Fauré

N° 4
Kitty-Valse

Nº 4
Kitty - Valse

250   Gabriel Fauré

N° 5
Tendresse

Nᵒ 5
Tendresse

SECONDA

256   Gabriel Fauré

Nº 6
Le pas Espagnol

Gabriel Fauré

Nᵒ 6
Le pas Espagnol

Cresc.

pp subito.

SECONDA

264   Gabriel Fauré